Volume VIII
Report No. 89
February 1974

Misuse of Psychiatry in the Criminal Courts: Competency to Stand Trial

Formulated by the
Committee on Psychiatry and Law

Group for the Advancement of Psychiatry

This publication was produced for the Group for the Advancement of Psychiatry by the Mental Health Materials Center, Inc., New York.

Additional copies of this GAP Publication No. 89 are available at the following prices: 1-9 copies, $3.00 each; 10-24 copies, list less 15 per cent; 25-99 copies, list less 20 per cent; 100-499 copies, list less 30 per cent.

Upon request the Publications Office of the Group for the Advancement of Psychiatry will provide a complete listing of GAP titles currently in print, quantity prices, and information on subscriptions assuring the receipt of new publications as they are released.

Orders amounting to less than $5.00 must be accompanied by remittance. All prices are subject to change without notice.

Please send your order and remittance to: Publications Office, Group for the Advancement of Psychiatry, 419 Park Avenue South, New York, New York 10016.

Standard Book Number 87318-124-7

Library of Congress Catalog Card Number 62-2872

Printed in the United States of America

TABLE OF CONTENTS

This is the tenth in a series of publications comprising Volume VIII. For a list of other selected GAP publications, see page 922.

STATEMENT OF PURPOSE

THE GROUP FOR THE ADVANCEMENT OF PSYCHIATRY has a membership of approximately 300 psychiatrists, most of whom are organized in the form of a number of working committees. These committees direct their efforts toward the study of various aspects of psychiatry and the application of this knowledge to the fields of mental health and human relations.

Collaboration with specialists in other disciplines has been and is one of GAP's working principles. Since the formation of GAP in 1946 its members have worked closely with such other specialists as anthropologists, biologists, economists, statisticians, educators, lawyers, nurses, psychologists, sociologists, social workers, and experts in mass communication, philosophy, and semantics. GAP envisages a continuing program of work according to the following aims:

1. To collect and appraise significant data in the field of psychiatry, mental health, and human relations;
2. To reevaluate old concepts and to develop and test new ones;
3. To apply the knowledge thus obtained for the promotion of mental health and good human relations.

GAP is an independent group, and its reports represent the composite findings and opinions of its members only, guided by its many consultants.

MISUSE OF PSYCHIATRY IN THE CRIMINAL COURTS: COMPETENCY TO STAND TRIAL *was formulated by the Committee on Psychiatry and Law. The members of this committee as well as other committees and the officers of GAP are listed below.*

COMMITTEE ON PSYCHIATRY AND LAW*
Alan A. Stone, Cambridge, Chr.
Edward T. Auer, St. Louis
John Donnelly, Hartford
Jay Katz, New Haven
Zigmond M. Lebensohn, Washington, D. C.
A. Louis McGarry, Brookline, Mass.
Seymour Pollack, Los Angeles
Gene L. Usdin, New Orleans
Andrew Watson, Ann Arbor

* Since formulation of this report, the Committee on Psychiatry and Law has changed personnel as follows: Carl P. Malmquist is currently serving as chairman, while Alan A. Stone has remained as a member of the Committee; Jay Katz, Zigmond M. Lebensohn and Andrew Watson have withdrawn to become Contributing Members of GAP; and Loren H. Roth has joined the Committee as a new member.

Committee on Adolescence
Joseph D. Noshpitz, Washington, Chr.
Warren J. Gadpaille, Englewood, Colo.
Charles A. Malone, Philadelphia
Silvio J. Onesti, Jr., Boston
Jeanne Spurlock, Nashville
Sidney L. Werkman, Denver

Committee on Aging
Robert N. Butler, Washington, Chr.
Charles M. Gaitz, Houston
Alvin I. Goldfarb, New York
Lawrence F. Greenleigh, Los Angeles
Maurice E. Linden, Philadelphia
Robert D. Patterson, Lexington, Mass.
F. Conyers Thompson, Atlanta
Prescott W. Thompson, San Jose, Calif.
Montague Ullman, Ardsley, N.Y.
Jack Weinberg, Chicago

Committee on Child Psychiatry
Joseph M. Green, Tucson, Ariz., Chr.
E. James Anthony, St. Louis
James M. Bell, Canaan, N.Y.
Harlow Donald Dunton, New York
John F. Kenward, Chicago
John F. McDermott, Jr., Honolulu
Exie E. Welsch, New York
Virginia N. Wilking, New York

Committee on the College Student
Robert L. Arnstein, Hamden, Conn., Chr.
Harrison P. Eddy, New York
Malkah Tolpin Notman, Brookline, Mass.
Gloria C. Onque, Pittsburgh
Kent E. Robinson, Towson, Md.
Earle Silber, Chevy Chase, Md.
Tom G. Stauffer, White Plains, N.Y.

Committee on the Family
Joseph Satten, San Francisco, Chr.
C. Christian Beels, Bronx, N.Y.
Ivan Boszormenyi-Nagy, Wyncote, Pa.
Murray Bowen, Chevy Chase
Henry U. Grunebaum, Boston
Margaret M. Lawrence, Pomona, N.Y.
David Mendell, Houston
Carol Nadelson, Boston
Norman L. Paul, Cambridge
Israel Zwerling, Bronx, N.Y.

Committee on Governmental Agencies
Paul Chodoff, Washington, D.C., Chr.
William S. Allerton, Richmond
Albert M. Biele, Philadelphia
Sidney S. Goldensohn, Jamaica, N.Y.
John E. Nardini, Bethesda, Md.
Donald B. Peterson, Fulton, Mo.
Harvey L. P. Resnik, Chevy Chase, Md.
Harold Rosen, Baltimore

Committee on International Relations
Bryant M. Wedge, Washington, D.C., Chr.
Francis F. Barnes, Chevy Chase
Eric A. Baum, Cambridge
Eugene Brody, Baltimore
Alexander Gralnick, Port Chester, N.Y.
Rita R. Rogers, Torrance, Calif.
Bertram H. Schaffner, New York
Mottram P. Torre, New Orleans
Roy M. Whitman, Cincinnati
Ronald M. Wintrob, Hartford

Committee on Medical Education
Saul I. Harrison, Ann Arbor, Chr.
Raymond Feldman, Boulder, Colo.
David R. Hawkins, Charlottesville
Harold I. Lief, Philadelphia
John E. Mack, Chestnut Hill, Mass.
David S. Sanders, Los Angeles
Robert Alan Senescu, Albuquerque, N.M.
Bryce Templeton, Philadelphia
Paul Tyler Wilson, Bethesda, Md.

Committee on Mental Health Services
W. Walter Menninger, Topeka, Chr.
Allan Beigel, Tucson, Ariz.
H. Keith H. Brodie, Menlo Park, Calif.
Eugene M. Caffey, Jr., Washington, D.C.
Merrill T. Eaton, Omaha
Archie R. Foley, New York
James B. Funkhouser, Richmond, Va.
Robert S. Garber, Belle Mead, N.J.
Stanley Hammons, Frankfort, Ky.
Donald Scherl, Boston
Jack A. Wolford, Pittsburgh

Committee on Mental Retardation
Henry H. Work, Washington, D.C., Chr
Howard V. Bair, Parsons, Kans.
Stuart M. Finch, Ann Arbor

Leo Madow, Philadelphia
George Tarjan, Los Angeles
Warren T. Vaughan, Jr., Burlingame, Calif.
Thomas G. Webster, Washington, D.C.

COMMITTEE ON PREVENTIVE PSYCHIATRY
Stephen Fleck, New Haven, Chr.
Frederick Gottlieb, Sherman Oaks, Calif.
Benjamin Jeffries, Harper Woods, Mich.
Ruth W. Lidz, Woodbridge, Conn.
E. James Lieberman, Washington, D.C.
Mary E. Mercer, Nyack, N.Y.
Harris B. Peck, Bronx, N.Y.
Marvin E. Perkins, White Plains, N.Y.

COMMITTEE ON PSYCHIATRY AND RELIGION
Sidney Furst, Bronx, N.Y., Chr.
Stanley A. Leavy, New Haven
Richard C. Lewis, New Haven
Earl A. Loomis, Jr., Greenport, N.Y.
Albert J. Lubin, Woodside, Calif.
Mortimer Ostow, Bronx, N.Y.
Bernard L. Pacella, New York
Michael R. Zales, Greenwich, Conn.

COMMITTEE ON PSYCHIATRY AND SOCIAL WORK
Alexander S. Rogawski, Los Angeles, Chr.
C. Knight Aldrich, Charlottesville, Va.
Maurice R. Friend, New York
John A. MacLeod, Cincinnati
Herbert C. Modlin, Topeka
John C. Nemiah, Boston
Charles B. Wilkinson, Kansas City, Mo.

COMMITTEE ON PSYCHIATRY IN INDUSTRY
Clarence J. Rowe, St. Paul, Chr.
Spencer Bayles, Houston
Thomas L. Brannick, Imola, Calif.
Duane Q. Hagen, St. Louis
R. Edward Huffman, Asheville, N.C.
Herbert L. Klemme, Topeka
Alan A. McLean, New York
David E. Morrison, Topeka
John Wakefield, Los Gatos, Calif.

COMMITTEE ON PSYCHOPATHOLOGY
Charles Shagass, Philadelphia, Chr.
Aaron T. Beck, Wynnewood, Pa.
Wagner H. Bridger, Bronx, N.Y.
Sanford I. Cohen, Boston
Daniel X. Freedman, Chicago
Paul E. Huston, Iowa City
Jack H. Mendelson, Boston
Richard E. Renneker, Los Angeles
George E. Ruff, Philadelphia
Albert J. Silverman, Ann Arbor, Mich.
George E. Vaillant, Cambridge, Mass.

COMMITTEE ON PUBLIC EDUCATION
Miles F. Shore, Boston, Chr.
Leo H. Bartemeier, Baltimore
Mildred Mitchell Bateman, Charleston
Robert J. Campbell, New York
James A. Knight, New Orleans
John P. Lambert, Katonah, N.Y.
Norman L. Loux, Sellersville, Pa.
Peter A. Martin, Southfield, Mich.
Mabel Ross, Chicago
Julius Schreiber, Washington, D.C.
Robert H. Sharpley, Brookline, Mass.
Robert A. Solow, Beverly Hills
Kent A. Zimmerman, Berkeley

COMMITTEE ON RESEARCH
Morris A. Lipton, Chapel Hill, Chr.
Stanley E. Eldred, Belmont, Mass.
Louis A. Gottschalk, Irvine, Calif.
Donald F. Klein, Glen Oaks, N.Y.
Ralph R. Notman, Brookline, Mass.
Alfred H. Stanton, Wellesley Hills, Mass.
Eberhard H. Uhlenhuth, Chicago

COMMITTEE ON SOCIAL ISSUES
Roy W. Menninger, Topeka, Chr.
Viola W. Bernard, New York
Roderic Gorney, Los Angeles
Lester Grinspoon, Boston
Joel S. Handler, Evanston, Ill.
Judd Marmor, Los Angeles
Peter B. Neubauer, New York
Perry Ottenberg, Merion Station, Pa.
Kendon W. Smith, Piermont, N.Y.
Raymond G. Wilkerson, Chicago

COMMITTEE ON THERAPEUTIC CARE
Robert W. Gibson, Towson, Md., Chr.
Bernard Bandler, Boston
Thomas E. Curtis, Chapel Hill
Harold A. Greenberg, Silver Spring, Md.
Milton Kramer, Cincinnati
Orlando B. Lightfoot, Boston
Melvin Sabshin, Chicago
Robert E. Switzer, Topeka

Committee on Therapy
Justin Simon, Berkeley, Chr.
Henry W. Brosin, Tucson, Ariz.
Peter H. Knapp, Boston
Eugene Meyer, Baltimore
Robert Michels, New York
Andrew P. Morrison, Cambridge
William C. Offenkrantz, Chicago
William L. Peltz, Manchester, Vt.
Franz K. Reichsman, Brooklyn
Lewis L. Robbins, Glen Oaks, N.Y.
Richard I. Shader, Newton Centre, Mass.
Harley C. Shands, New York
Joseph P. Tupin, Sacramento
Herbert Weiner, Stanford, Calif.

Contributing Members
Carlos C. Alden, Jr., Buffalo
William H. Anderson, Springfield, Ill.
Charlotte G. Babcock, Pittsburgh
Grace Baker, New York
Walter E. Barton, Washington, D.C.
Anne R. Benjamin, Chicago
Ivan C. Berlien, Coral Gables, Fla.
Sidney Berman, Washington, D.C.
Grete L. Bibring, Cambridge
Edward G. Billings, Denver
Carl A. L. Binger, Cambridge
H. Waldo Bird, St. Louis
Wilfred Bloomberg, Boston
Peter W. Bowman, Pownal, Me.
Matthew Brody, Brooklyn
Ewald W. Busse, Durham
Dale Cameron, Geneva, Switzerland
Norman Cameron, Tucson, Ariz.
Gerald Caplan, Boston
Hugh T. Carmichael, Washington, D.C.
Jules V. Coleman, New Haven
Robert Coles, Cambridge
Harvey H. Corman, New York
Frank J. Curran, New York
Robert S. Daniels, Cincinnati
William D. Davidson, Washington, D.C.
Leonard J. Duhl, Berkeley
Lloyd C. Elam, Nashville
Joel Elkes, Baltimore
Joseph T. English, New York
Louis C. English, Pomona, N.Y.
O. Spurgeon English, Narberth, Pa.
Jack R. Ewalt, Boston
Dana L. Farnsworth, Boston
Malcolm J. Farrell, Waverley, Mass.
Alfred Flarsheim, Chicago
Alan Frank, Albuquerque, N.M.
Moses M. Frohlich, Ann Arbor
Daniel H. Funkenstein, Boston
Albert J. Glass, Chicago
Milton Greenblatt, Boston
Maurice H. Greenhill, Scarsdale, N.Y.
John H. Greist, Indianapolis
Roy R. Grinker, Sr., Chicago
Ernest M. Gruenberg, Poughkeepsie, N.Y.
Edward O. Harper, Cleveland, Ohio
Mary O'Neill Hawkins, New York
J. Cotter Hirschberg, Topeka
Edward J. Hornick, New York
Joseph Hughes, Philadelphia
Portia Bell Hume, Berkeley
Irene M. Josselyn, Phoenix
Jay Katz, New Haven
Sheppard G. Kellam, Chicago
Marion E. Kenworthy, New York
Ernest W. Klatte, Santa Ana, Calif.
Gerald L. Klerman, Boston
Othilda M. Krug, Cincinnati
Zigmond M. Lebensohn, Washington, D.C.
Henry D. Lederer, Washington, D.C.
Robert L. Leopold, Philadelphia
Alan I. Levenson, Tucson, Ariz.
David M. Levy, New York
Reginald S. Lourie, Washington, D.C.
Alfred O. Ludwig, Boston
Jeptha R. MacFarlane, Westbury, N.Y.
Sidney G. Margolin, Denver
Helen V. McLean, Chicago
Karl A. Menninger, Topeka
James G. Miller, Washington, D.C.
John A. P. Millet, New York
Kenneth J. Munden, Memphis
Rudolph G. Novick, Lincolnwood, Ill.
Lucy D. Ozarin, Bethesda, Md.
Irving Philips, San Francisco
Charles A. Pinderhughes, Boston
Vivian Rakoff, Toronto
Eveoleen N. Rexford, Cambridge
Milton Rosenbaum, Bronx, N.Y.
W. Donald Ross, Cincinnati
Lester H. Rudy, Chicago
Kurt O. Schlesinger, San Francisco
Elvin V. Semrad, Boston
Calvin F. Settlage, Sausalito, Calif.

1

INTRODUCTION

During the past decade a growing segment of American society has begun to distrust the decision-making processes of government. Much of this distrust is aimed at the courts which administer our system of criminal justice. Conservatives distrust the courts because, in their view, recently proposed procedural technicalities favor the criminal element, whereas minority groups distrust these courts because, in their view, there is bias and prejudice throughout the system detrimental to minority members of the society.

Against this background there has been an upsurge of interest in the role of psychiatrists in the decision-making process of these courts.[1] As one might expect, conservatives see the psychiatrists as tipping the balance still further in favor of the criminal, while minority groups and some liberals have begun to assert that "psychiatric justice" implements prejudice and bias.

This report will examine that facet of the decision-making process where the system of criminal justice requires the collaboration of psychiatrists. It is the conviction of the Committee on Psychiatry and Law that this one facet is important in itself, but seen from the larger viewpoint it is crucial because it is illustrative of the broader range of problems which contribute

[1] Thomas Szasz. LAW, LIBERTY AND PSYCHIATRY (New York: Macmillan, 1963); and Nicholas Kittrie. THE RIGHT TO BE DIFFERENT (Baltimore, Md.: Johns Hopkins Press, 1972).

to what has become a major domestic crisis in American life—distrust of the decision-making process.

Distrust of judicial decision-making is an issue whenever the court acts with wide powers of discretion. Often in the exercise of his discretion the judge will turn to the psychiatrist for the latter's opinion. This is most apparent in the juvenile court system and in cases where mental illness is an identified question, but it is also encountered in the disposition of all criminal cases in which decisions about probation and length of sentence are made with considerable discretion and often on the basis of information supplied by psychiatrists and social workers.

On those few occasions when psychiatrists have thought seriously about their role in the decision-making process of criminal justice, their focus has been on the insanity defense. Yet, as one legal commentator has suggested, the incidence of cases in which the insanity defense is raised is lower than the annual incidence of poisonous snakebites on the island of Manhattan.[2] The far more common but neglected role of psychiatrists in the system of criminal justice is that of helping the court decide whether a defendant is competent to participate in the trial which will determine his guilt or innocence. This is one of those "low visibility" aspects of the decision-making process which characteristically goes on without a jury, without public awareness, without clear legal or psychiatric standards, and often without adequate legal counsel for the defendant.

But neglect of this important problem rests not only on the shoulders of the psychiatric profession—the legal profession has been equally ignorant and unaware. Lawyers, judges, and many existing state laws confuse the two separate questions [3]

[2] Fred Cohen. Review of A. Goldstein's "Insanity defense," *Contemporary Psychology* 13, 8 (1968): 386. There are a few jurisdictions in which for a variety of reasons the insanity defense is a fairly frequent phenomenon, e.g., Washington, D. C., and California. Cf. Arthur J. Matthews, Jr., MENTAL DISABILITY AND CRIMINAL LAW (New York: American Bar Foundation, 1970. See especially pp. 26 ff, "Quantitative data on criminal responsibility cases."

[3] Travis Lewin, "Incompetency to stand trial: Legal and ethical aspects of an absurd doctrine," *Law & Social Order* (Arizona State law journal) 19, 1 (1969): 233-265.

which require psychiatric testimony: (1) Is this defendant *competent* to participate in a trial to determine his guilt or innocence? (2) Is this defendant participating in a trial *responsible* for the criminal acts of which he has been accused?

To underline the importance of the former question, which is the subject of this report, consider the fact that the majority of persons now held in institutions for the criminally insane are there not because they have been found not guilty by reason of insanity, but rather because they were judged incompetent to participate in a trial and therefore have never been tried on the question of their guilt or innocence. In many instances decades have passed since the alleged crime occurred, and thus these defendants await a trial which it would no longer be feasible to hold for both legal and practical reasons.

As one surveys the demeaning and degrading conditions which exist in hospitals for the criminally insane, the awful hypocrisy of our society and its system of criminal justice stands revealed in the harsh light of reality. American psychiatry, if for no other reason than its passive complicity in this situation, must share the burden of social responsibility for it. These defendants, who are presumed innocent until proved guilty, are forced to live in circumstances far worse than those imposed on convicted murderers. Statistics document the extent of these abusive practices. In 1962, of those patients held at Matteawan State Hospital for the criminally insane in New York State, 65.5 percent were there because they were found incompetent to stand trial; whereas 0.5 percent were there because they had been found not guilty by reason of insanity.[4]

Morris reviewed the statistics at Matteawan in 1968 after significant legal reform had halved the population of that institution. He found that 78 percent of the patient-inmates were categorized as incompetent to stand trial.[5] A Michigan study reveals the same pattern. Research covering a ten-year period

[4] Thomas Szasz, PSYCHIATRIC JUSTICE (New York: Macmillan, 1968), page 50.
[5] Grant Morris, The confusion of confinement syndrome extended: The treatment of mentally ill "noncriminal criminals" in New York, *Buffalo Law Review* 18 (1968-69): 393-413.

from 1956 to 1966 revealed that 849 patients had been committed to the Ionia State Hospital as "criminally insane." Of that number, more than 90 percent were defendants found incompetent to stand trial.[6]

The comprehensive survey compiled by the Joint Information Service of the American Psychiatric Association confirms these studies, with the finding that 52 percent of all admissions of mentally ill offenders are incompetent to stand trial, and 4 percent are not guilty by reason of insanity.[7]

Although data about the fate of incompetents are incomplete, Hess and Thomas reported in 1963 that more than 50 percent of those found incompetent to stand trial would "spend the rest of their lives confined to the hospital."[8] This impression has been substantiated in a recent report by McGarry.[9]

These data lead to the inescapable conclusion that the low-visibility decision of incompetence is far more significant in practical terms than is the high-visibility decision of not guilty by reason of insanity. As the psychiatrist looks at the data, he must, of course, consider whether the process of such decision-making, despite its low visibility, may not in fact produce correct and reasonable outcomes. For example, one might well conclude that where the question of mental illness of an alleged criminal arises, the illness in most cases will be so profound that it affects both the defendant's competency to stand trial and his responsibility for the alleged crime. Since in Anglo-American law the question of competency is generally raised before that of sanity, most profoundly mentally ill defendants

[6] J. P. Acher, R. Guzman & T. H. Lewin, PSYCHIATRIC EVALUATION IN CRIMINAL CASES (Ann Arbor: Michigan Department of Mental Health, March 1967).

[7] P. L. Scheidemandel & C. K. Kanno, THE MENTALLY ILL OFFENDER: A SURVEY OF TREATMENT PROGRAMS (Washington, D. C.: Joint Information Service, APA-NIMH, 1966).

[8] J. H. Hess & H. E. Thomas, Incompetency to stand trial: Procedures, results and problems, *American Journal of Psychiatry* 119 (1963): 713-720.

[9] A. L. McGarry, The fate of psychiatric offenders returned for trial, *American Journal of Psychiatry* 127 (Mar. 1971): 1181-1184.

will be diverted from the adjudicative process at the early point.[10]

This argument will in fact stand up under the test of logic and of empirical data, but such confirmation only underlines the greater pragmatic importance of the result of the incompetency finding. It suggests an imperative need to make the criteria for decision-making which lead to a finding of incompetency more visible to the general public and more comprehensible if we are to restore confidence in the decision-making process. At the same time, if one were to focus solely on the initial decision-making process, it would leave unanswered questions which it must be the prime responsibility of psychiatrists to answer, namely, what treatment does the defendant who is found incompetent receive, and what effect does the finding of incompetency have on his capacity to regain his mental health?

These are vital questions to which the Committee will return, but it may be helpful first to illustrate these complex matters by the time-tested device of psychiatry and of law—the case method.

[10] McGarry, *op. cit.* at note 9 preceding.

2

DUSKY v. UNITED STATES

The particular case to be reported had great legal significance. On appeal it reached the Supreme Court, whose members articulated what have become the federal criteria of competency to stand trial. The Committee has included as part of this case history a dialogue between judge and psychiatrist which emphasizes the conflicting assumptions that confound communication across disciplines.

Competency to stand trial:

Dusky v. United States [11]

Milton Richard Dusky, then 33 years of age, was charged by an indictment filed September 10, 1958, with having unlawfully transported and caused to be transported in interstate commerce from Johnson County, Kansas, to Ruskin Heights, Missouri, on or about August 19, 1958, a certain girl who had been unlawfully kidnapped, carried away, and not liberated unharmed —all in violation of 18 USC § 1201.

The female victim was a 15-year-old high school student who lived with her parents in Ruskin Heights, a suburb of Kansas City, Missouri. About noon on August 19, 1958, she was walking to a neighborhood drugstore to have lunch with another girl. Dusky, with two boys, Leonard Dischart, age 14,

[11] *Dusky v. United States,* 271 F 2d 385 (8 Circ 1959); *Dusky v. United States,* 362 U S 402 (1960) (per Curiam); and *Dusky v. United States,* 295 F 2d 743 (8 Circ 1961).

and Richard H. Nixon, age 16, drove by in Dusky's automobile and offered her a ride to the drugstore. Although she did not know Dusky, she had met Nixon before and she knew Dischart casually. She accepted the ride. After Dusky and the two boys left her at the drugstore, they went to the nearby Wheel Inn Drive-In. There they drank vodka supplied by Dusky and discussed the girl—what kind of girl she was and whether they could have sexual relations with her. They returned to the drugstore and waited for her.

When she came out of the drugstore, they offered to drive the girl home. She refused, but when they asked again as she started to walk up the highway, she accepted. They did not take her home, but first pretended to be going to another girl's home, which they passed before driving into the neighboring state of Kansas. Dusky was driving, but after they passed the other girl's home Dischart took the wheel. They then stopped on a back road where, with a small knife displayed, the two boys raped her. Dusky also attempted to have intercourse with her, but was unsuccessful. Dusky drove them all back to Ruskin Heights and to the Wheel Inn Drive-In, where the girl was permitted to leave the car to get a drink of water. She ran into the place and told one of the employees that she had been attacked.

The FBI agent who arrested Dusky and Dischart the next evening subsequently testified as to Dusky's competency to stand trial. He reported that when he told Dusky he had a federal warrant for his arrest on the charge of kidnapping, Dusky said, "That's a pretty serious crime, isn't it?" Dusky had then inquired what the charge referred to, and the agent told him, "It refers to the incident where you all picked up that girl out in Ruskin Heights the day before," to which the defendant replied, "That wasn't kidnapping—she got in the car voluntarily."

Dusky's attorney found it difficult to consult with his client, and despite the FBI agent's testimony at Dusky's arraignment on this charge of kidnapping, requested that he be committed to the Federal Medical Center at Springfield, Missouri, for examination to determine his competency to stand trial. After Dusky spent four months at the medical center, a court hearing was held. It should be noted that the psychiatrist who testified at this hearing was a federal employee and not someone hired by the defense attorney. The hearing evoked a psychiatric history containing the following information:

> Mr. Dusky was reared in "severely traumatic circumstances" and suffered all his life from feelings of inadequacy. He had been grossly maladjusted since childhood. He was discharged from the Navy because of psychoneurosis, and subsequently twice hospitalized in VA hospitals. A third hospitalization in a nonmilitary facility was the result of a suicidal attempt. His various symptoms led to a divorce and he had been able to achieve no pattern of stable object relations. He had used alcohol in large quantities and over an extended period of time in a symptomatic fashion.
>
> Psychological testing in the hospital indicated "inadequacy, anxiety, impulsiveness, poor reality contact, lack of ego strength, auditory and visual hallucinations," etc. During his stay at the Federal Medical Center he had episodes of paranoid ideation and ego disruption, particularly when medication was stopped. The diagnosis agreed upon by the government psychiatrist and psychologist was schizophrenic reaction, chronic undifferentiated type. Despite this long history and despite the gravity of the diagnosis, the defendant's mental status was not grossly impaired if his Thorazine dosage was adequately regulated.

When the government psychiatrist was questioned on the stand, he indicated that Dusky understood the charges against him and comprehended the powers of the court, but argued that Dusky could not assist his attorney in his own defense. The psychiatrist, after being questioned by both attorneys, was subjected to an interesting line of inquiry from the judge.[12] This

[12] Matthews, *op. cit.* at note 2.

hearing differed from similar hearings in that the judge, the psychiatrist, and the lawyers all understood the distinction between the insanity defense and the question of competency to stand trial. The questioning is therefore on point and it reveals some of the typical contrasts in professional approach as between disciplines, for example:

1—The case history. For the psychiatrist it is the basis for his search for the meaning and causes of the individual's current behavior. For the judge it is an exculpatory self-serving alibi to be challenged and/or documented by corroborating evidence.

2—Symptoms. For the psychiatrist they are the typical manifestations of mental illness. For the judge they are questionable constructs of significance only when all commonsense explanations can be discounted.

3—Mental capacity. For the psychiatrist this term is a global one including many aspects of mental condition. For the judge it is a matter of cognition and memory.

4—Mental illness. For the psychiatrist it is a system of classification for purposes of treatment and prognosis. For the judge it is a label that confuses the legal questions.

5—Tranquilizers. For the psychiatrist they are a treatment modality. For the lawyers they are substances which alter the mind of the defendant and confuse the evaluative decision of the court.

In the court excerpt that follows, *Judge J* is the judge, *Dr. A* the psychiatrist, *Mr. D* the defense attorney, and *Mr. P* the prosecuting attorney:

Judge J: Doctor, let me ask you some questions. Is your opinion based in large fashion on the facts that are shown in these two reports?

Dr. A: The reports, Judge, Your Honor, reflect a summarization of the findings at the time they are made and also in the initial study of the evidence, the information obtained from the patient; and from whatever source he can get it, which is agencies and so on, the hospitals where he might have been hospitalized; and it does not convey the full picture in the words we can try to convey it, to attempt to communicate what we see and hear and believe about this man.

Judge J: Now, in this report . . . there is a lot of factual information concerning his wife, his family, his parents, and then . . . some detailed information concerning the circumstances surrounding the offense. Doctor, where did you get that information?

Dr. A: That information came from the patient. We have no factual information of the circumstances of his offense.

Judge J. So that he was able to tell you certain background information of his own family life and some detailed information concerning the night before and day of the alleged offense?

Dr. A: Yes.

Judge J: Do you have any reason to believe that the information given to you and reported in that paragraph is not factually accurate?

Dr. A: I do in that at times this man has varied his story from this a little bit. I will say in essence, though, that this information is probably as near as the information he could give us would be accurate. We do have a communication from his wife which adds to it and verifies it somewhat.

Judge J: Yes. Now, as to the details of the circumstances leading up to the alleged offense and immediately before it, what information do you have that demonstrates a variation from this report that you have here, except that he from time to time varied his story?

Dr. A: I am not quite sure—are you asking how he varied his story?

Judge J: Yes, in the particular circumstances involved in this offense, how has he varied his story? You said you questioned the veracity of it because he varied it from time to time.

Dr. A: Yes. In the beginning Mr. Dusky could not tell us very much about this, but as he stayed in the institution, he began to remember a little more about it, and then I think this is the result of giving him some medication to [the point] where his anxiety and his tension and fear were somewhat alleviated. Then we tried him without giving him medication and he became much worse, could not clarify, not only could not clarify, but in telling some of the circumstances, he volunteered the information that it was a part of a plot to get him and that these boys were doing things to protect themselves and put all the blame on him, and the circumstances were not the same as they had been described in the original report. I am sorry but I don't have the story outlined specifically clear in my mind other than in terms of delusional thinking that occurred at this time with reference to persecution.

Judge J: Do you consider any suggestion made by a person committing a crime that someone else is trying to shift the blame from themselves to him evidence of insane delusion?

Dr. A: No, I do not. That is pretty common.

Judge J: It is quite common in the ones we deal with, of course. What I am trying to do is to develop in my own mind, if I can, from your testimony and from your study of this man in what particular thing he is, by his past conduct with you, demonstrating an inability to work with his counsel in preparing some sort of a defense to this charge. Let me predicate that question by making this statement, that we are not concerned in this finding with whether he is so insane as to be unable to distinguish between right and wrong.

Dr. A: I understand.

Judge J: What we are concerned with is solely the question whether or not he is unable to understand the proceedings against him or properly, under those circumstances, to work with his counsel in preparing a defense, whether it is a defense based on insanity or any other grounds. Now, with that preliminary as to the information I want, I would like you to point out to me why, under the circumstances, he would be unable to assist his counsel in preparing a defense to this particular charge.

Dr. A: First, this man is mentally ill. His illness is—

Judge J: Well, now do I understand that you subscribe to the premise that simply because a man is mentally ill . . . he is unable to work with his counsel in preparing a defense to a charge that might be against him?

Dr. A: Not just the fact that he is mentally ill, but the character of his mental illness.

Judge J: All right. Elaborate on that a little.

Dr. A: The character of this man's mental illness is such that his thinking is distorted. He does not have realistic thinking; he is unable to add two and two, figuratively speaking, and come up with a proper conclusion.

Judge J: We are not concerned with conclusions now. We are concerned with whether or not he knows that this figure is two, and this figure is two. One of the reasons he has attorneys is to arrive at the proper total of four. Now, let's don't talk for the moment about his ability to reach conclusions. Let's talk about his ability to recite facts.

Mr. D: Your Honor, may I submit at this point that Your Honor has asked the doctor a question, namely, you asked upon what he bases his conclusion that the man is unable properly to assist in his defense, and the doctor started to say, number one, mental illness, and then he was going on with some other thing, and I would like to have Your Honor hear from the witness his complete answer to your question.

Judge J: All right. I don't develop it properly with my line of questioning, you do it but, Mr. D, I am trying to follow a line of thinking now that I have, which may or may not be proper, but it is information that I want to develop, and I am not going to restrict any of you in your examination or cross-examination or recross-examination, or whatever it is. What I am trying to do is to form a conclusion based on this and any other testimony that may be presented here, and in my own way I am trying to develop some thoughts that I have. Whether they are right or wrong remains to be seen. Now, will you read the question again? Let's go back.

[The last question, by the Court prior to the colloquy, was thereupon read.]

Dr. A: Your Honor, in interpreting facts, which we understand as facts, the statement of the patient that this might be a fact might not be true because of his distorted thinking, his defective reasoning and judgment, and his inability to interpret realistically anything which is going on. That doesn't apply to everything, but there are certain areas, which I am unable to define accurately, just where his thinking is distorted other than in the terms of delusions and hallucinations as part of his mental illness.

Judge J: Now getting back to your starting premise, to go back where Mr. D. wanted us to go back a few minutes ago, you said that one reason why he was not, in your opinion, capable of properly assisting in his own behalf was the fact that he was mentally ill.

Dr. A: Yes.

Judge J: Now, what else?

Dr. A: This was in terms—I was going to then define what I meant as far as his mental illness is concerned—

Judge J: All right.

Dr. A: . . . that it affects his reasoning, his judgment, his interpretation of what is going on about him, and his ability to answer questions and respond to his attorney or others as a witness. This man's statement cannot be taken to be factual when he is unable to differentiate reality from unreality.

Judge J: Well, now, getting back to the conversations you have had with him as basis for formulating your opinion here about his mental illness as it relates to the precise incident which furnishes the basis of this charge, what statements did he make to you that might demonstrate to us his inability to describe those circumstances and those events?

Dr. A: Your Honor, my examination, opinion and interpretation about this man is based very little on the circumstances of the offense. We discussed the offense and he told me what he could tell me from time to time. It came out during other conversations. But most of my contacts with this man have been in the form of discussing the actual environmental things at Springfield and his feeling, his thinking, his lifetime story and so forth. So that very little of the actual decisions that I have made in my own mind are based on information relative to the offense. In other words, when this man tells me that we have a microphone in his room behind the radiator by which we are calling him bad names, this is not concerned with the offense [in any way] whatsoever; this is part of my mental examination and interpretation of the mental illness, which is of such severity that he is unable to reason or interpret accurately.

Judge J: Did you reach the conclusion as a result of your series of tests of him that, in general, he was able to distinguish between right and wrong?

Dr. A: I was unable to clearly differentiate that.

Judge J: Did you make any particular effort to determine that particular element?

Dr. A: I did not. We have no verified factual information about the events whatsoever.

Judge J: As a matter of fact, you are not concerned particularly, are you, Doctor, about the legal definition of insanity, that is, the ability to determine right from wrong?

Dr. A: I am not concerned?

Judge J: Yes.

Dr. A: I am concerned to the degree that the Court has asked me, or the United States Attorney has asked me, to give consideration to this question and to try to give an opinion about it. I tried, I know, as a consultant to the Court in the capacity in which I am able. I didn't have any information on which I could develop an opinion referable as to whether he knew the difference between right and wrong at that time.

Judge J: You couldn't determine from just talking to him?

Dr. A: No, sir.

Judge J: Now, I notice you have here in this report a statement that the evening before this incident occurred, defendant had taken some Thorazine, which had been issued to him during his last commitment to the Veterans Administration Hospital, and that he wandered around town. I take it that you got this information from him?

Dr. A: Yes, sir. The sentence started off, he said he took Thorazine.

Judge J: And then the next instance, during the night he said he drank about two pints of vodka. During the following day he continued to drink heavily.

Dr. A: Yes.

Judge J: Entirely aside from anything else, those two matters might well explain the conclusion in the third paragraph down that he denied complete memory of the events on the day of the alleged offense?

Dr. A: He could have been drunk at the time and not remember and this is why he said he didn't remember the events.

Judge J: He was at this date, and in your opinion I believe you testified, still is oriented as to time, place and person?

Dr. A: Yes.

Judge J: He realizes he is in court today, he realizes that he was down there pursuant to a Court order for psychiatric examination?

Dr. A: Yes.

Judge J: He knows who his attorney is, he knows what he is charged with having done?

Dr. A: Yes.

Judge J: And to some extent, at least, he knows some, or expresses a knowledge of some, of the incidents leading up to the commission of the offense that he is alleged to have committed?

Dr. A: Yes, sir. He resents having been ejected from his rooming house, I believe it was the night before, that he and his boy were put out on the street; I think they slept in his car the night before the incident occurred. This was his story to me. There is great emotional disturbance over this incident. His boy was accused of having disturbed his landlady. Now, he was angry at the landlady for having accused his son, wherefore he was responsible, whereas the other children were all right; he feels very disturbed about failing this boy. I mentioned there was a great deal of emotional turmoil going on right at that time.

Judge J: All right. I believe that is all. Thank you, Doctor. Mr. D, you can inquire further, or you can, Mr. P, or both of you.

Mr. D: Just one further question. Doctor, in the course of four months that you have been treating and examining this patient, Mr. Dusky, have you found it necessary, from time to time, and particularly as stress and strain would come upon him, to administer drugs and medication to this patient?

Dr. A: I have. He has been on drugs almost continuously. We always, before we review a case with the staff, remove the medication in order to see the basic symptomatology that is present. When this man was taken off medication he became so ill that we were concerned. We felt a little—that we could almost not wait until the staff meeting where he was to be seen before we got him back on medication because he was so agitated, so emotionally tense, so restless—all the symptoms were so greatly exaggerated.

Mr. D: Doctor, in your profession do you have a professional medical opinion and psychiatric opinion as to whether or not, under the stress and strain of trial for kidnapping, the man would have to be subjected to drugs, and if he were tried at this time, the administration of drugs?

Dr. A: I can only say that he requires medication and I am sure that under any stress, such as a trial, he would require additional medication.

Mr. D: Thank you. I have no further questions.

Redirect examination

Mr. P: Would you be more specific, Doctor, as to what medication you refer to.

Dr. A: These are tranquilizing drugs which are widely used in mental illness.

Mr. P: They do not have the effect of being so strong or having such an effect on him that he doesn't know what is going on or anything of that kind—don't put him in a stupor or anything of that sort, do they?

Dr. A: No, sir, on the contrary, he is better able to answer questions and better able to respond when less agitated, less disturbed and [in] less turmoil with these medications. However, I think it would be unfair to say that this is the man's basic personality as long [as] he is on medication.

Mr. P: But if he were on medication he would be better capable of assisting his attorney and the defense of the case and so on, is that correct?

Dr. A: This I cannot answer directly because maybe his attorney's defense would be better when he is at his worst.

Mr. P: I see what you are getting at, but what I mean is a better understanding of what is going on in the courtroom.

Dr. A: Yes.

Mr. P: He will understand and realize better if he is under the influence of these drugs?

Dr. A: Yes.

Mr. P: In other words, what I am trying to get at—if he is administered these tranquilizing drugs during the trial, this will not be like being under the influence of a heavy course of hypnotics?

Dr. A: No, sir.

Mr. P: Being completely out if the case should be tried. For instance, we have had cases where someone has claimed he was not really aware of the proceedings and so forth because he was under narcotics at the time of trial. That would not be the case here?

Dr. A: No, sir.

Mr. P: All right. What is Thorazine he claims to have taken, when? The night before the offense?

Dr. A: The chemical name is chlorpromazine. Chlorpromazine is a tranquilizer and Thorazine is the name of the particular drug this drug company puts out.

Mr. P: Then in that event he would probably be more nearly normal than if he had not taken it?

Dr. A: I don't like to use the word "normal." I think he would be less agitated, less concerned. It might be he was so unconcerned he didn't particularly care what he did. In other words, this is one thing a tranquilizer does: A man who has illusions, hallucinations—they are very disturbing to him. He takes tranquilizing drugs—he knows these illusions are disturbing him and he takes tranquilizing drugs and they do not disturb him so much.

Mr. P: I think that is all.

Judge J: I think that is all, Doctor. Thank you very much.

[Witness excused.]

Mr. P: We have no further testimony. I think the defendant should have an opportunity to testify if he so desires.

Mr. D: The defense rests on the Doctor's testimony, Your Honor, and desires to offer no further evidence at this hearing.

Judge J: Well, I am disappointed about that because I had hoped to get some assistance in formulating my views based on the defendant's own explanation. I am not going to insist on it, although there is a complete bar to the use of the defendant's testimony in the trial on its merits. However, in the absence of the defendant's own testimony, I am forced to conclude that since this is not a hearing on whether or not the defendant is insane as it is interpreted to excuse criminal conduct, I am of the opinion that the evidence developed thus far, showing as it does that the defendant is oriented as to time and place and person, understands the nature of the charge that is pending against him, understands that he is actually being charged with an offense, understands what that offense is and as far as his ability to recite facts is concerned, in my opinion is able properly to assist in his own defense to the extent that he can develop those facts with his own attorney, it is my conclusion that he properly should be kept here and not returned to the Medical Center, and that he is competent to stand trial in the narrow sense of that term as used under Section 4244. That is not in any way saying, gentlemen, that he is responsible, as not being mentally incompetent, for the offense for which he is being tried. It is simply in the narrow test that is used in the hearing under Section 4244 of Title 18. Since he is oriented as to time and place and person; since he, in my opinion, based on the limited evidence that has been presented so far, is able to assist counsel in his own defense, then it will be concluded that he is mentally competent to stand trial and will be retained here until the case is set for trial.

Mr. D: Your Honor, may the record show my objection and exception to the Court's ruling in view of the undisputed testimony of the Government's witness, the psychiatrist, the Government psychiatrist, that he is not properly able to assist in his defense and I, as his attorney, have reached that same conclusion, although I do not feel, as his attorney, that I should take the witness stand and be sworn and offer evidence in that regard. I make this statement as a lawyer to the Court and I believe that the man is not properly able to assist his counsel in his defense and should not be tried at this time.

Judge J: Mr. D, of course you may note your exception and it may go in the record. However, may I suggest to you that if we used the general test of mental incompetency that is proper in defenses based on that ground, [no one] who was suffering from some mental illness of a severe nature could ever be brought to trial in the Federal court under this section. As I understand the narrow scope of the hearing contemplated under Section 4244, it simply is an action for us to determine whether he is sufficiently oriented as to time, place and person, and if he has a sufficient amount of background facts that he can work with counsel, the question of his ultimate mental capacity to commit the offense is one that we are not passing on at this time.

After this hearing affirming his competency to stand trial, Dusky's first trial took place in March 1959. His principal defense was insanity. He was found not insane, was convicted and sentenced to a 45-year jail term by the district court.

Dusky's lawyer appealed this conviction [13] (reported at 271 F2 385); error was asserted as to the trial court's finding that the defendant was competent to stand trial, and as to issues relating to the insanity defense. The Court of Appeals, how-

[13] *Dusky v. United States* 271 F 2d 385 (8 Circ 1959).

ever, affirmed the conviction and subsequently appeal was made to the Supreme Court of the United States.

The Supreme Court reversed the conviction and remanded the case to the district court "for a new hearing to ascertain petitioner's present competency to stand trial, and for a new trial if petitioner is found competent." [14] The Court stated that the test for competency which must be met is whether the defendant *"has sufficient present ability to consult with his lawyer with a reasonable degree of rational understanding—and whether he has a rational as well as a factual understanding of the proceedings against him."* [15]

The required new hearing to ascertain Dusky's competence to stand trial took place October 3, 1960, the testimony produced following the guidelines of the Supreme Court's test. At that time psychiatric testimony established Dusky as then competent, and his defense counsel acknowledged that he was not then experiencing the difficulty in consulting and working with his client which he had encountered at the time of the first trial.

Rearraignment followed immediately. A plea of not guilty by reason of insanity was again entered and the new trial took place on October 4, 1960. Dusky was again found guilty over his insanity defense, and a lighter sentence of 20 years was imposed, with the possibility of parole after 5 years.[16]

[14] *Dusky v. United States* 362 U S 405 (1960) (per Curiam).
[15] *Ibid.*
[16] *Dusky v. United States* 295 F 2d 743 (8th Circ 1961). Dusky is now on parole from that sentence.

3

THE PROBLEMS RAISED BY THE DUSKY CASE

The Dusky case highlights a range of problems which must be considered and which are discussed in the sections that follow. First of all, where do the legal standards of competence come from, and what purpose do they serve? Second, what are the modern legal criteria of competence? Third, how can psychiatric information be incorporated into those standards? Fourth, what is the effect of most tranquilizers in current use on a defendant's competence to stand trial? Fifth, what is the ethical justification for a psychiatrist's depriving a patient of medically prescribed drugs necessary for his health in order to help a court make a legal determination?

Defendant referral to psychiatric facilities

Before dealing with these problems it is instructive to consider how defendants like Dusky are initially referred to psychiatric facilities. Empirical data on this subject can be found in a fascinating report published by the Michigan Department of Mental Health,[17] and we have supplemented these data out of our own pooled clinical experience. The issue of a defendant's competency is unlike most other legal issues in that the initial question can be raised by the judge, by the prosecutor, or by the defense. Indeed, based on *Pate v. Robinson*,[18] a recent Supreme Court decision, each of these participants has a re-

[17] Acher, Guzman & Lewin, *op. cit.* at note 6.
[18] *Pate v. Robinson* 383 U S 375 (1966).

sponsibility to raise the question. The Michigan study, confirmed by our own data, reveals how, during the time of the study, attorneys on both sides react to this responsibility.

What first became apparent was the seemingly arbitrary manner in the way one prosecutor operated as opposed to another, a difference which in reality depends on a variety of conditions. For example, in some counties in Michigan, the competency examination was apt to be quite expensive if performed by psychiatrists brought to the jail, and the cost was borne by the county. This led some prosecutors and many judges to avoid it. When a psychiatric facility was routinely available without extra cost—as it was, for example, in Detroit—it was used much more often.

Surprisingly, some prosecutors raised the question of competence as a favor to defense counsel. That is, defense counsel may decide his client is quite disturbed, but either the defendant cannot be convinced to raise the issue, or defense counsel is constrained out of fear or anxiety to mention it. Counsel then turns in desperation to his supposed adversary for help.

When the prosecutor decides to press charges and to go forward with a criminal trial, a number of questions arise which relate to his discretion—for example, if the crime was bizarre, or if the defendant is obviously hallucinated and deluded—is so disturbed that even a lay person can tell that something is wrong—then the prosecutor may want to get just enough information to help him reach a decision. He may prefer not even to go ahead with a trial that involves such an outlay of time and money if he can be assured that the defendant is truly mentally ill and will be confined for treatment. At the time this study was conducted, however, under the Michigan law and that of other states, only two courses of action were available to him. He would either have to request an examination for competency so as to get a psychiatric opinion, or proceed to trial.

Often the prosecutor will be quite willing to drop charges

or suggest probation when he can be certain the defendant will be hospitalized, but in a case of this kind he cannot be certain of this, nor can he reassure the victim or the victim's family when he cannot be certain that a lengthy civil commitment will follow. In such a situation the prosecutor will often request a competency hearing to get some clue both as to subsequent legal strategy and as to how he might best use his prosecutorial discretion. If he goes ahead with his request for determination of competency, he can rest assured that the defendant will not be let out on bail.

When we examine this pattern of prosecutorial use of the competency determination, it is hard to argue that the prosecutor is intentionally and maliciously exploiting his powers. Often, it seems, he is simply protecting himself and the community as he thinks in the best interest of all, but the fact is that what he does in these cases he simply could not do in ordinary criminal cases, and his additional power derives from his raising the specter of mental illness.

Of course the prosecutor must convince a judge that the examination is necessary, but there seems to be no legal standard defining the word *necessary* in this context. Indeed, the Committee's own clinical experience suggests that judges have quite different thresholds on this question. Some judges seem to use the competency examination as a punitive measure or as a device to preclude the possibility of bail. This often seems to be the case in states where competency examinations take place in maximum-security institutions over a long period of time under demeaning living conditions. Other judges will order competency examinations for the sake of completeness in cases which they expect to be controversial. Most common, perhaps, is the practice of using competency in a supposedly humanitarian fashion for a variety of those chronic problems, like alcoholism, which plague the criminal courts.

Defense attorneys make use of the question of competency for a variety of reasons depending on tactical considerations and personal experience. Lawyers who feel strongly that the conditions of confinement involved are demeaning may conceal obvious problems or, in ambiguous situations, lean in the direction of ignoring the question. A poll of defense attorneys in Michigan [19] revealed that 20 percent admitted to having concealed the issue of incompetence one or more times. In one case [20] defense counsel was criticized for ignoring the question by the Judge: "The defense attorney's failure to raise the defense was reprehensible and constituted a denial of effective assistance." Defense attorney testified that he considered ten years in prison a better outcome than life at the state institution for the criminally insane.

If their clients are indigent and they can obtain psychiatric data for an insanity plea only by raising the question of competency, defense attorneys will do so. But the judgment of the defense lawyer as to his client's competency has a special significance (as indicated in the Dusky case), since one of the criteria is the ability of the defendant to consult with his lawyer. Different lawyers will have different standards and different tolerance levels for evaluating the ability of their client to consult with them.

It has been the clinical impression of this Committee that some lawyers deal particularly well with emotionally disturbed clients and feel comfortable about representing them. Other lawyers expect very little collaboration from their clients and thus, depending on the facts of the case, they may want little or no consultation with them. At times, defense attorneys will abuse the competency examination themselves by utilizing it as a device to delay trial, whether because they believe delay will help their case, or because delay offers the busy lawyer a welcome postponement of a potentially laborious trial.

In general, competency referral can best be conceptualized as one part of a network of legal procedures through which

[19] Acher, Guzman & Lewin, *op. cit.*, at note 6.
[20] *Evans v. Kropp* 254 F Supp 318 (E D Mich 1966).

authority attempts to control and confine behavior socially defined as deviant (sick). Where legal authority is deprived by legislative reform of broad capacity to invoke civil commitment for deviant behavior it may well turn to other devices like determination of competency. This is illustrated by the recent developments in California, where one of the side effects of new, more limited civil commitment laws has been the court's use of competency referral at an unprecedented rate.[21]

Judicial commitment of the mentally ill was no longer easily accomplished in California after 1970 as a consequence of the Lanterman-Petris Mental Health Act of 1969. Prior to 1970 many mentally ill defendants from municipal courts of Los Angeles County were dealt with by being judicially committed as mentally ill persons for care and treatment in state mental hospitals and their criminal charges were either suspended or dismissed. After 1970 *this* disposition was no longer available to the courts; however, judicial commitment of the mentally ill defendant charged with a crime and held mentally incompetent to stand trial was still available. Therefore, in order to provide treatment for these mentally ill defendants, the court found them mentally incompetent to stand trial and then committed them for treatment on that basis. During the calendar year of 1969, Metropolitan State Hospital received a total of 20 such committed defendants largely from the Los Angeles County municipal courts. During 1970 the number of defendants committed as mentally incompetent to stand trial had risen to 600. Almost all of these mentally ill defendants were either returned to court as mentally competent to stand trial or their criminal charges were dismissed within three months after their having been committed.

These abuses involving the request for a competency examina-

[21] H. V. Petris, Judge, LA County Superior Court, Psychiatric Department: THE LANTERMAN-PETRIS-SHORT ACT; ITS PROCEDURES AND PROBLEMS. Report to the California Superior Court Workshop (Oct. 24, 1969) Fairmont Hotel, San Francisco; and S. Pollack, Panel Psychiatrist, LA County Superior Court, personal communication.

tion would have only limited significance were it not for what the statistics presented earlier indicate: that once found incompetent, a defendant is very likely to remain for the rest of his life in an institution for the criminally insane. (Some states have already attempted to avoid this unfortunate situation—for example, Massachusetts, New York, California, Michigan, and the District of Columbia. However, such states are still a minority.) To understand this unhappy development, we turn to the historical background of the competency standard and to the questions raised by the Dusky case.

4

HISTORICAL AND CURRENT STANDARDS FOR COMPETENCY

Background of legal standards for competence

Historically, the legal problem of competency had both a ritual and a fairness function. The ritual function arose in connection with an attempt by the early English courts (which had quasi-religious overtones) to deal with a procedural problem. At that point in the trial when the defendant was supposed to plead guilty, on rare occasions he would stand mute. The problem for the court was to decide whether the defendant was "mute by visitation of God" or "mute of malice." [22] The ritual aspects of the trial required that the defendant verbalize some type of plea. If he could not or would not, the entire system of justice was temporarily thrown into disarray. An early remedy to facilitate court procedure was the *peine forte et dure* [23] (performed without the collaboration of psychiatrists) in which the defendant was slowly crushed with heavier and heavier weights in the hope that his endurance would eventually give out and he would perhaps gasp out some type of plea. Of course he might die in the process, which would also dispose of the case.

In addition to serving the ritual requirements of the trial,

[22] A. J. Robertson, THE LAWS OF THE KINGS OF ENGLAND, EDWARD TO HENRY I (Cambridge, England: Cambridge University Press, 1925).
[23] Nigel Walker, CRIME AND INSANITY IN ENGLAND, Vol. 1, THE HISTORICAL PERSPECTIVE (Edinburgh, Scotland: Edinburgh University Press, 1968).

competency had a fairness or protective function. It expressed an overriding concern that the defendant be able to protect himself in the context of the Anglo-American trial system in which he and his attorney are seen as taking on the prosecution in an adversary struggle.

The standards for incompetency emerged out of a series of celebrated trials [24-26] held in the 18th and 19th centuries (Appendix A). These standards emphasized cognitive capacity of the defendant to understand the procedures and collaborate with his attorney, but there is little evidence that psychiatrists were familiar with these standards. Instead, psychiatrists seem to have applied the standards of certifiability (civil commitment) with which they were familiar.

These vague standards, so ambiguously applied, were brought to the United States, where in our legal system they have continued to function with the same degree of confusion. Nonetheless, as we analyze the function of the competency question in American criminal courts today, the historical principles of *ritual* and *protection of the defendant* are still what emerge as the expressed goals of this legal doctrine.

Legal purposes of competency to stand trial

Legal commentators have emphasized certain principles as underlying competency to stand trial: [27]

1) To safeguard the accuracy of any criminal adjudication. At the minimum, accuracy of the proceedings requires that the accused be able to provide his counsel with facts necessary to make possible an adequate defense. This is especially critical where the accused is the only person in possession of exonerating factual material.

2) To guarantee a fair trial. A basic sense of humanitarian

[24] STATE TRIALS, edited by T. B. Howell, Vol. 22, LONDON, 1809-26, page 307.
[25] *Regina v. Dyson,* Carrington & Payne 305: 1 Lewin 64 (1931).
[26] Nigel Walker, *op. cit.* at note 23 (page 227).
[27] An excellent review and analysis of the legal commentary (Incompetency to Stand Trial) is to be found in *Harvard Law Review* 81 (1967): 454-473.

fairness requires that a person be aware of what is happening in a criminal proceeding so that he can take all steps open to him in protecting himself from the possible consequences of the trial. In order to make certain basic decisions concerning selection of counsel and determination of plea, the accused must have some understanding of the nature of the proceedings and his role in them.

3) To preserve the integrity and dignity of the legal process. "If a defendant attempts to conduct his defense in a bizarre manner, his behavior may destroy the decorum of the court. And even if defendant remains passive, his lack of comprehension fundamentally impairs the functioning of the trial process. The adversary form of the criminal proceeding necessarily rests on the assumption that defendant will be a conscious and intelligent participant; the trial of a defendant who cannot fulfill this expectation appears inappropriate and irrational. The adjudication loses its character as a reasoned interaction between an individual and his community and becomes an invective against an insensible object." [28] This third consideration links the problem of competency to stand trial with the recent highly publicized episodes of courtroom disruption (e.g., in the Manson and Sirhan trials).

4) *To be certain that the defendant, if found guilty, knows why he is being punished.* A significant element in the meaning and justification for punishment is retribution. That element is lost on the defendant who does not understand the reason for his imprisonment.

These principles underlying the requirement of competency give heavy emphasis to protection of the defendant. It is therefore ironic, as we have already documented, that the finding of incompetency may well result in the worst possible outcome for the defendant—a lifetime sentence to a hospital for the criminally insane.

[28] *Ibid.*, page 458.

Current legal standards for competency

In the introduction to this report the difficulties inherent in the issue of competency to stand trial were in large part attributed to legal confusion. This is demonstrated in the following quotation from the most recent encyclopedic study by the American Bar Foundation:

> The exact state of mind required for the postponement of criminal proceedings has been variously phrased in state statutes, but few of them lay down an explicit test such as appears in proceedings to establish criminal irresponsibility. Whatever the statutory formulation of the tests of present competency, most jurisdictions have retained the common-law criteria of ability to comprehend the proceedings and ability to assist in the defense as interpretive guidelines for the statutory language. However, statutory terminology turns out to be a source of confusion: The competency provisions of most states speak only in terms of "insanity," or insanity in conjunction with terms denoting other inapposite mental conditions such as idiot, lunatic, unsound mind, imbecile, mentally deranged, and so forth.[29]

Thus, lawyers and psychiatrists who turn to the statute for guidance may be led to suppose that incompetency equals insanity. Since most psychiatrists equate psychosis with insanity, we can assume that modern practice is little advanced beyond that we have described as prevailing in nineteenth century England.

If we turn to appellate decisions which interpret the statutes in light of specific cases, we get little additional enlightenment. The federal standard articulated by the Supreme Court in *Dusky v. U.S.* adds little to the common-law language cited above. The Dusky standard was expressed as follows: "The test must be whether he [defendant] has sufficient present ability to consult with his lawyer with a reasonable degree of

[29] Samuel J. Brakel & Ronald S. Rock, THE MENTALLY DISABLED AND THE LAW, Rev. ed. (Chicago, Ill.: University of Chicago Press, 1971. *Copyright © 1961, 1971, by the American Bar Foundation. All rights reserved*), page 410.

rational understanding, and whether he has a rational as well as factual understanding of the proceedings against him." [30]

The Supreme Court, however, failed to define *a reasonable degree* of rational understanding. If we look to appellate cases in the state court for such definitions, we find considerable variation. Thus, in Massachusetts a defendant lobotomized by a self-inflicted gunshot wound was found competent to stand trial, since he was considered "sufficiently a human being though impaired to appreciate the peril of his position. . . ." [31] On the other hand, in a leading case in Iowa, a defendant is incompetent to stand trial if he is "so mentally deranged *as not to appreciate exactly* the nature of the criminal charge against him." [32]

Based both on published research and on the Committee's experience in attempting to work with these vague standards, it becomes obvious that a new legal standard with more precise definitions is required. This is a task for lawyers. Unfortunately the Model Penal Code prepared by the prestigious and reform-oriented American Law Institute does little but reiterate the common-law standard: "No person who as a result of mental disease or defect lacks capacity to understand the proceedings against him or to assist in his own defense shall be tried. . . ." [33] etc.

Ideally, the finding of competency or incompetency to stand trial is a legal fact which is supposed to be arrived at (once the issue is raised), by a judge or—in a few jurisdictions, a jury—functioning as finders of fact based on the evidence placed before them and weighed against a precise standard articulated by statute or appellate courts. Because the law is vague and imprecise, the judge's decision may be difficult, but that is the court's problem and they must wrestle with it themselves.

[30] *Dusky v. United States, op. cit.*, at note 14.
[31] *Commonwealth v. Harrison* 343 Mass 279, 173 N E 2d 87 (1961).
[32] *State v. Bruntlett* 36 N W 2d 450, 240 Iowa 338 (1949).
[33] MODEL PENAL CODE (Proposed official draft, 1962), § 4.04, Comment (Tentative Draft No. 4, 1955).

The psychiatrist can best perform his function if he presents relevant information to the court without himself attempting to relieve the court of its difficult legal question. Although he ought not attempt to decide the legal question, the psychiatrist must realize that the information he provides can only be relevant if he keeps in mind the common-law standard despite its vagaries.

5

INCORPORATING PSYCHIATRIC INFORMATION INTO COMPETENCY STANDARDS

The common-law standard is two-pronged: On the one hand it includes capacity of defendant to consult with his attorney and, on the other, capacity to understand the proceedings against him. This means that the question of competency might or might not be raised, depending on legal counsel and his interpersonal skills in relating to defendant and developing a defense. It may be that a given mentally ill defendant would be competent with one attorney but incompetent with another.[34] It is also true that the complexity of the facts of the case—whether a complex embezzlement or a tax fraud as opposed to a simple theft; or, more generally, whether felonies as opposed to misdemeanors—requires very different levels of functioning on the part of the defendant. Finally, it is clear that similar mental pathology may have a differing impact on the competency of different defendants.

All these variables suggest that the competency test is more related to the particulars of the anticipated trial than most psychiatrists have recognized. Thus there is probably *no single standard of competency* in contrast to *the single standard of criminal responsibility*.

Fortunately a few forensic psychiatrists have recognized these

[34] E. J. Balcanoff & A. L. McGarry, Amicus curiae: The role of the psychiatrist in pretrial examinations, *American Journal of Psychiatry* 126 (1969): 342-347.

problems and have attempted to identify the kinds of information that will be helpful to the courts by assembling a variety of checklists for this purpose (see Appendix B). One of these checklists attempts both (1) to be comprehensive of all possible criteria for a legal finding of incompetency and (2) to make possible the quantification of degrees of capacity (or incapacity) of the criteria listed.[35]

Because the question of competency uniquely relates to the specific legal context, sophisticated approaches have necessarily highlighted specific legal desiderata of competency. This means that the psychiatrist must have some elementary familiarity with the criminal process in order to conduct a meaningful examination. Such familiarity, however, can rapidly be attained *de novo* if the psychiatrist reviews one of these checklists with the attorney involved or with the judge. Indeed, one of the chief values of these checklists is that they allow productive collaboration between professionals having no interdisciplinary experience.

The impairment of mental functions of concern in this legal determination can be understood in psychiatric perspective as a matter of ego dysfunction. Impairments of ego functions should be clearly identified and described in a manner comprehensible to the nonpsychiatrist.

It may be helpful for the psychiatrist to set the problem of competency before himself in this way: After a careful psychiatric examination, he might ask himself, has mental illness or disease affected the patient's mental status such that it would in some general way interfere with his understanding of the legal issues? his capacity to recall and disclose significant information? his ability to consult and communicate with his lawyer? Psychiatric conditions relevant to these broadly stated questions would include the following:

[35] A. L. McGarry, "Competency to Stand Trial and Mental Illness," in CRIME AND DELINQUENCY ISSUES, an NIMH Monograph Series, DHEW Publication # (HSM) 73-9105 (Rockville, Md.: DHEW).

1) Impaired clarity of sensorium
2) Reduced level of alertness
3) Impaired orientation
4) Inadequate memory (incapacity for recognition, retention and recall, impairment of recent memory and remote memory)
5) Specific psychiatric syndrome(s) such as depression, delirium, mental retardation
6) Specific psychiatric symptom(s) such as delusions, illusions, hallucinations
7) Thought disorders as evidenced by autism, poverty of thought, paranoid ideas, bizarre dereistic thoughts
8) Abnormalities in thought progression, such as flight of ideas, peculiar associations, bizarre expressions
9) Abnormalities in affect and mood as evidenced by profound anxiety, severe depression, or extreme emotional dyscontrol with inconsistency and inappropriateness in affect
10) Inadequacy of conative and volitional behavior as evidenced by dyscontrol of executive ego functions in negativism, mutism, and marked incapacity to control motor behavior

This psychiatric information will in part be the product of interview data, which are affected by transference-countertransference reactions; by the value system of the psychiatrist; and by the role the patient thinks the physician has been assigned.

Having spelled out the psychiatric data in traditional terms and in relation to attributes of competency, the psychiatrist should then attempt to become more specific by asking himself how these impairments, if present, affect the defendant's capacity in relation to the various legal desiderata that must be taken into consideration. The checklists summarized below can be utilized in several ways to answer these questions. They may be used at some point in the actual assessment as the basis for a structured interview.[36, 37] They may be used as a framework for the psychiatrist's report to the court. Some research has been done in attempts to incorporate these legal desiderata into the psychiatric framework of ego functions and mental status in order to produce a standardized device or instrument which would supplement or perhaps even replace a psychiatric examination.[38]

The criteria itemized in these checklists [39] and testing instruments [40] depend heavily on the defendant's cognitive awareness, but also on his emotional capacity to cooperate with his lawyer and on his general affect. Although the itemization may create the sense in the naive reader that enormous legal sophistication is required of both psychiatrist and defendant, this is by no means the case. The specific items in these checklists have included the following (see also Appendix B): the defendant's ability—

1—to understand his current legal situation
2—to understand the charges against him
3—to understand the facts relevant to his case
4—to understand the legal issues and procedures in his case
5—to understand legal defenses available in his behalf
6—to understand the dispositions, pleas, and penalties possible
7—to appraise the likely outcomes
8—to appraise the roles of defense counsel, the prosecuting attorney, the judge, the jury, the witnesses, and the defendant
9—to identify and locate witnesses
10—to relate to defense counsel
11—to trust and to communicate relevantly with his counsel
12—to comprehend instructions and advice

36 Barry A. Bukatman, J. L. Foy & Edward Degrazia, What is competency to stand trial? *American Journal of Psychiatry* 127 (1971): 1225-1229.
37 P. D. Lipsitt, D. Lelos & A. L. McGarry, Competency for trial: A screening instrument, *American Journal of Psychiatry* 128 (1971): 105-109.
38 A. L. McGarry, *op. cit.*, at note 35.
39 Bukatman, Foy & Degrazia, *op. cit.*, at note 36; and Ames Robey, Criteria for competency to stand trial. Presented at the 121st Annual Meeting of the American Psychiatric Association, 1965.
40 A. L. McGarry, *op. cit.*, at note 35.

13—to make decisions after receiving advice
14—to maintain a collaborative relationship with his attorney and to help plan legal strategy
15—to follow testimony for contradictions or errors
16—to testify relevantly and be cross-examined if necessary
17—to challenge prosecution witnesses
18—to tolerate stress at the trial and while awaiting trial
19—to refrain from irrational and unmanageable behavior during the trial
20—to disclose pertinent facts surrounding the alleged offense
21—to protect himself and to utilize the legal safeguards available to him

Some of these criteria overlap, but on the whole they reflect a valuable attempt to relate the data obtained in the psychiatric examination to the trial situation.

Psychological test results can also be of value in supporting the clinical findings of mental impairment and in directing the psychiatrist to areas of function he may have misunderstood or misinterpreted. He should not be intimidated by the apparent legal complexity of the checklist items. All of them can easily be clarified by a discussion with the judge or the defense attorney.

There remains a problem in predicting the defendant's future behavior. That is, he may pass the "tests" relating to present cognitive awareness, but it is difficult to determine how he may function at the time of the trial (as suggested in item 18 above). His future ability to satisfy the competency standards spelled out in these checklists and testing instruments will be affected by changes in his clinical status, and will in part be determined by the external situation during the trial as modified by the understanding and sensitivity of his defense counsel and the court. The psychiatrist should state what clinical safeguards will be necessary if the patient is to remain mentally competent to stand trial, with reference to the use of drugs, return to hospital between court sessions, continued psychiatric treatment, and the like.

Occasionally the psychiatrist must evaluate the defendant, otherwise mentally competent to stand trial, who cannot work "meaningfully" with defense counsel; or the mentally ill defendant who may be mentally competent with one counsel and incompetent with another. A responsible psychiatrist should attempt to remedy an ineffective defendant-attorney relationship by consultation either with the attorney, or conjointly with attorney and defendant.

The reports of a competency evaluation should address the standards itemized in the above checklist and should indicate what criterion presently poses, or in future might pose, a problem. The report should contain sufficient data to justify the conclusions reached and to indicate how they were reached. These conclusions should not set forth an opinion as to whether the defendant is legally competent. The data offered, however, will enable the Court to assume its proper responsibility and make an enlightened legal judgment as to the defendant's competency.

> *Note.*—A minority opinion of this committee holds that when the psychiatrist testifies in court his responsibility is to the social-legal system, and that he is the agent of society in this setting. Therefore, he must be familiar with the legal concepts of competency to stand trial; he must relate his clinical findings to the pertinent legal question; and he should offer, on the basis of clinical findings, an opinion concerning the ultimate issue to be determined by the court.
>
> This minority position holds that the forensic psychiatrist's primary responsibility is to apply his psychiatric material to the social ends of legal justice, rather than to the specific needs of the individual patient. A corollary to this viewpoint considers that the properly trained forensic psychiatrist directs himself to the legal conclusions from his initial entry into the arena of litigation and, therefore, that the forensic psychiatrist should offer his opinion on the ultimate legal question.

> These positions are subject to considerable dispute and are being hotly debated today. Although the Committee majority opts for the position traditionally associated with the role of physicians, the opposing point of view is well expressed in the literature.[41]

A special clinical problem for the psychiatrist exists in the case of defendants who claim amnesia. The symptoms of amnesia can be the product of brain injury, psychological disorder, or the defendant's malingering. The differentiation of the last two is a modern version of the problem which confronted the early English judges, "mute by visitation of God" or "mute of malice." In a recent opinion, one court has decided that the presence of amnesia—whether physical, psychological, or feigned—may not render the defendant incompetent to stand trial, depending on the circumstances of the case.

In *Wilson v. United States*[42] the defendant suffered from retrograde amnesia which was the result of brain damage incurred in an auto accident as he left the scene of the crime. Judge J. Skelly Wright concluded that with certain limitations the trial nonetheless could be held.[43]

> A prediction of the amnesic defendant's ability to perform these functions essential to fairness and accuracy must, of course, be made before trial at the competency hearing. But where the case is allowed to go to trial, the trial judge should determine at its conclusion whether the defendant has in fact been able to perform these functions. Before imposing sentence he should make detailed written findings (after taking any additional evidence deemed necessary) concerning the effect of the amnesia on

[41] Seymour Pollack, M.D., "Psychiatric Consultation for the Court," in THE PSYCHIATRIC CONSULTATION, edited by W. Mendel & P. Solomon (New York: Grune & Stratton, 1968); and "Principles of Forensic Psychiatry for Psychiatric-Legal Opinionmaking," in LEGAL MEDICINE ANNUAL, 1971, C. Wecht, Ed. (New York: Appleton-Century-Crofts, 1971).

[42] *Wilson v. United States* 391 F 2d 460 (D.C. Circ 1968).

[43] *Ibid.* pp. 463-464. "The accused must be able to perform the functions which 'are essential to the fairness and accuracy of a criminal proceeding.'" [*Pouncey v. United States,* 121 U S App D.C. 264, 266, 349 F 2d 699, 701 (1965).]

the fairness of the trial. In making these findings the court should consider the following factors:

1. The extent to which the amnesia affected the defendant's ability to consult with and assist his lawyer.

2. The extent to which the amnesia affected the defendant's ability to testify in his own behalf.

3. The extent to which the evidence could be extrinsically reconstructed in view of the defendant's amnesia. Such evidence would include evidence relating to the crime itself as well as any reasonably possible alibi.

4. The extent to which the Government assisted the defendant and his counsel in that reconstruction.

5. The strength of the prosecution's case. Most important here will be whether the Government's case is such as to negate all reasonable hypotheses of innocence. If there is any substantial possibility that the accused could, but for his amnesia, establish an alibi or other defense, it should be presumed that he would have been able to do so.

6. Any other facts and circumstances which would indicate whether or not the defendant had a fair trial.

After finding all the facts relevant to the fairness of the trial, considering the amnesia, the court will then make a judgment whether, under applicable principles of due process, the conviction should stand.

6

PSYCHOACTIVE DRUGS AND COMPETENCY TO STAND TRIAL

It is the contention of this committee that the vast majority of defendants currently found incompetent to stand trial could rapidly be returned to competence and so maintained were the facilities and treatments of modern psychiatry made available to them. Of primary importance in this situation is the use of psychoactive drugs. During the early 1960s there was considerable judicial confusion about the facts of drug treatment which had tragic consequences. Defendants relieved of acute psychotic symptoms by the use of major tranquilizers would be returned to local jails to await trial. There they languished without necessary drug treatment, which in many instances produced a reexacerbation of acute symptoms. The Michigan study previously cited reports a number of striking examples:

> One patient accused of killing her sister's children was committed to Ionia. . . . In late 1965 her condition had improved to the point where she was recommended for return to court. The Superintendent (of Ionia) advised the Court by letter that the defendant required drugs and set forth the prescription. The defendant remained in jail for over a month before being examined by a local psychiatric commission. During that month she was given no drugs and her condition deteriorated to the point where she began to hallucinate actively. Finally she attempted suicide by pouring lighter fluid on her hair and setting fire to it. She was returned to Ionia as still incompetent.[44]

[44] Acher, Guzman & Lewin, *op. cit.*, at note 6.

The reasons for this and similar tragic developments are directly attributable to the lack of intelligent collaboration between psychiatrists and jurists. The fault often lies with "institutional psychiatrists." Thus we find Dr. Charles E. Smith, Medical Director of the Bureau of Federal Prisons, writing as late as 1966 that:

> The use of tranquilizing medication has given rise to a new problem. These drugs are effective in improving the mental condition of many cases so that while receiving the drugs their condition is so improved that they may be regarded as competent. However, frequently such a patient will relapse if the medication is discontinued. Because of the problems involved in handling such cases in a trial proceeding, we have taken the position that it is *undesirable* to return them for further hearings so long as they required tranquilizing drugs. In all such instances thus far, the courts have supported this position.[45] (Italics added.)

The position taken by Dr. Smith would certainly be unconscionable if it were the policy followed by psychiatrists in the disposition of other patients suffering from mental illness. If no patient could be returned to society unless free of medication, the major revolution in psychiatric treatment accomplished by psychoactive medication would be virtually worthless. Why, then, should those patients found incompetent to stand trial be bound to a standard of improvement so arbitrary and in many cases impossible of fulfillment? In part the answer is to be found in the intransigence of the courts. Thus, one federal judge dealing with such a case stated: "I don't want to see this patient again until such time as he is competent without medication."[46] The judge may or may not have realized that he was in effect pronouncing a lifetime sentence.

The reaction of such judges was and is based on the false assumption that tranquilizing drugs produce a kind of "chemi-

[45] Charles E. Smith, Psychiatric Approaches to the Mentally Ill Federal Offender, *Ninth Circuit Sentencing Institute* 39 FRD 523, 560-561 (1966).
[46] Acher, Guzman & Lewin, *op. cit.*, at note 6.

cal sanity" which creates a state of mind unacceptable for participation in a trial.[47] Yet many persons in responsible positions throughout society function effectively despite their continued need for similar medication. Indeed, there is little doubt that some judges, attorneys and physicians are among this very group.

Two decades of clinical experience with psychoactive medication suggest that the Supreme Court of Louisiana was correct when in 1969 it concluded that: "A defendant whose mental capability was maintained only through use of a prescribed medication was competent to stand trial, and likelihood that defendant would relapse if use of medication was interrupted did not ban defendant from proceeding to trial." [48]

An inescapable problem which does result from the use of appropriate drugs to restore a defendant to competency is the fact that his physical appearance and demeanor in court may be affected by the drugs. These alterations may affect the jury's assessment of the reliability and significance of the defendant's testimony. The effect of drugs on the demeanor of the defendant is illustrated in *State v. Murphy*,[49] where the defendant was given three tranquilizers shortly before he took the witness stand. The drugs apparently enabled the defendant to appear calm, cool and detached as he related the gory details of the murder for which he was on trial. His courtroom demeanor on this occasion contrasted sharply with his prior appearance. The State of Washington Supreme Court reversed his conviction, stating that there was a "reasonable possibility that [the defendant's] attitude, appearance and demeanor, as observed by the jury, have been substantially influenced or affected by circumstances over which he had no real control." [50]

[47] M. H. Buschman & J. M. Reed, Tranquilizers and competency to stand trial, *American Bar Association Journal* 54 (1968): 284-287; and C. B. Scrignar, Tranquilizers and the psychotic defendant, *American Bar Association Journal* 53 (1967): 43-45.

[48] *State of Louisiana v. Eunice Hampton* 253 La 399, 218 La 2d 311.

[49] *State v. Murphy* 56 Wash 2d 761, 768, 355 P 2d 323, 327 (1960).

[50] *Ibid.*

The effect of this distortion of the defendant's demeanor might occur in any trial where drugs are used to restore and maintain the defendant's competency. The effect would have great legal significance in cases involving the insanity defense. The calm composure of the defendant made possible by drugs designed to restore and maintain his competency might sway a jury in its attempt to determine defendant's true mental state at the time of the crime.

This legally undesirable consequence of drug-induced demeanor can be minimized if the fact of the dependency of defendant's demeanor on drugs is known to the other trial participants. When in such circumstances a defendant appears in court, the judge and legal counsel for both parties should be told by the examining psychiatrists: (1) that the defendant is appearing under the influence of drugs; and (2) the type of drug administered the defendant, the dosage, and the effect the drug has had on the defendant's demeanor. This information should be admissible at the discretion of the defense attorney and the judge so that the jury can take this aspect of the defendant's demeanor into account when dealing with the insanity defense.[51] Excerpts from videotaped psychiatric interviews of the defendant before such treatment is initiated might be a useful device for establishing a base line in such cases. The practice observed in the Dusky case of withdrawing necessary medication simply for the purpose of evaluating competency is unreasonable in the opinion of this committee and perhaps unethical in light of current medical experience.

[51] *State v. Gwaltney* 77 Wash 2d 906, 468 P 2d 433 (1970).

7
CONCLUSIONS AND RECOMMENDATIONS

There are a variety of abuses which attend the legal procedures of competency to stand trial. Most of these abuses originate in the fact that lawyers caught up in the adversary process of the criminal law tend to exploit procedural devices to gain tactical advantage. Psychiatrists have unwittingly collaborated in these tactical maneuvers by losing sight of the fact that their primary responsibility is to their patients.

The purpose of this report has been to reveal the complexities and ambiguities of this low-visibility decision-making procedure and to offer guidance to psychiatrists so that they may find their way through the legal technicalities while asserting their primary function.

The most serious abuse of the competency procedure, however, concerns the result produced. All too frequently a determination of incompetence becomes a lifetime sentence to a hospital for the criminally insane. Such facilities rarely have adequate treatment available, and the patient's uncertainty about his future trial and its outcome adds a further and sometimes overwhelming obstacle to his possible improvement.

Legally this disposition seems to fly in the face of the basic tenets of criminal law by taking the defendant's liberty while denying him a trial. If the loss of liberty were compensated by adequate treatment, or if the period of confinement were limited, there might be some justification for this practice, but in most jurisdictions neither condition prevails. The abusive practices currently prevailing have no rational basis either in law or in psychiatry. This has been recognized by the Supreme Court in its recent important holding in *Jackson v. Indiana*.[52] There the incompetency finding would have led to the lifetime commitment of a nondangerous deaf mute with the I.Q. of a preschool child, and for whom no treatment was available.

Intelligent collaboration between courts of law and psychiatrists will be necessary to remedy these abuses. Toward this end, the Committee on Psychiatry and Law proposes the following new procedures which, to be effective, require new statutes and well-informed physicians and lawyers as participants in their proper execution:

1. Psychiatrists should screen every defendant whose competency is questioned, *before* he is transported to an institution for the criminally insane. Thus, when the issue of competence is initially raised, the psychiatrist can participate in the threshold question. This is particularly desirable when it is the prosecution or the court which raises the question of the defendant's competency. Statistics such as those from the Massachusetts Department of Mental Health for fiscal 1971 reveal that only 74 out of 1,806, or 4.1 percent of pretrial admissions to Massachusetts mental hospitals during this period resulted in findings of incompetency. These statistics more than suggest a need for screening examinations prior to such stigmatizing admissions.

In part, the decision to admit such a defendant to a psychiatric facility is inescapably a medical decision because the detention period is usually much longer than that required for diagnosis alone. Some treatment may and will be given, and the defendant will be exposed to an institutional environment which may or may not be medically appropriate. Psychiatrists should resist referrals for extensive diagnosis *or treatment,* even when they come from a court, unless they feel that there is a genuine psychiatric need for the treatment and stay involved.

[52] *Jackson v. Indiana* 406 U S 715.

A screening instrument such as that developed by McGarry's group may well provide valuable adjunctive data at this stage.[53]

2. Many of the persons found incompetent to stand trial by the court are not dangerous to themselves or to society. It is therefore inexcusable to continue their confinement in maximum-security institutions. Such nondangerous defendants, who would otherwise be eligible for bail, should be hospitalized or treated at the same hospitals and in the same manner as any other mental patient. The treatment should be that best calculated to restore the defendant's mental health as soon as possible. Where medically indicated, treatment should include outpatient care as well as hospitalization. The dangerous incompetent defendant who would not otherwise be bailable should if necessary be confined and treated in a maximum-security institution. If these recommendations were followed, maximum-security institutions might well become more effective because their patient census would be reduced by elimination of those incompetents who are currently confined without regard to the need for maximum-security detention.

3. It is the belief of this committee that new techniques and drugs currently available can bring most persons initially found to be incompetent to a competent state well within six months of initiation of treatment. At present, this is the maximum length of time normally required to treat most civilly committed patients in hospitals. After six months of treatment, the vast majority of all defendants originally adjudged incompetent will fall into one of two categories: (a) they will be competent to stand trial; or (b) they will be found to be suffering from a type of mental disability such as that due to gross mental retardation, brain damage, or some chronic deteriorated state which makes it possible for the psychiatrist to predict that the defendant will never regain competency. The first group, of course, should stand trial. Criminal charges against the second group should be dropped, and they should, instead, be subject

[53] Lipsitt, Lelos & McGarry, *op. cit.*, at note 37.

to commitment proceedings where their danger to society is reassessed and the type of institutionalization required, if any, is determined. Those persons who will never return to competency, and who pose no threat to themselves or the community, should be released.

4. There will be a small number of incompetency cases which do not fit into either of these categories. After six months of treatment these defendants will not be competent to stand trial, but it may not be clear that they can never return to competency. For these few, the judge should hold a hearing and, if indicated, grant a six-month extension of the initial treatment period. At the end of the extension period, comprising a total of twelve months' treatment, the defendant should be returned for trial or civilly committed to that institution best equipped to treat him.

Given the adversary background of the criminal law, these new procedures, the primary aim of which is to prevent abuse and allow for adequate treatment of the defendant, will themselves be tested and exploited. The nature of that exploitation might well prove to be similar to that described in the historical account of early English law in which a mute defendant was adjudged as "mute of malice." That is, criminal defendants charged with grave offenses may well attempt to malinger for 12 months on the expectation of escaping trial. Experience suggests that this may occur. However, simply to avoid such a possibility, it is unnecessary to retain our current system, which discourages malingering by permanently confining all defendants found incompetent in hospitals where living conditions are often worse than prison conditions.

As an alternative, this committee suggests the following: If the alleged crime is a serious felony, and the question of competency has not been resolved after one year, the court should have the discretion of retaining the criminal charges and its jurisdiction over the defendant, with the power to proceed to trial at some future time when and if the question of competency is resolved.

The maximum length of the delay should bear a reasonable relationship to the jail term applicable as the criminal penalty for the crime alleged.

Many of the reforms proposed by this committee could be implemented or initiated by psychiatrists even without passage of new statutes.

Psychiatrists who become involved in evaluating problems of defendant competency should take the following steps:

1. They should, whenever possible, attempt to participate in the initial screening process when the issue of competency is first raised.

2. Psychiatrists who occupy positions in hospitals for the criminally insane should take note of the fact that in many jurisdictions patients referred to them by the courts come with a provision allowing "no more than x number of days" of hospitalization. They can therefore within legal bounds examine the defendant-patient on the day of arrival and if a decision of competency can be reached at that point, he should be returned immediately to the court.

3. If the court finds the defendant incompetent, the psychiatrist should work against a deadline of six months of hospitalization. Recognizing that competency is a much lower standard than cure, the psychiatrist should aim at returning all such defendants to the court within a month or two. Certainly this task should take no longer than six months.

4. As soon as the psychiatrist decides it unlikely that the defendant will ever regain competency, he should so inform the court and the defendant's lawyer, at this time emphasizing that further confinement in that particular institution may be detrimental to the defendant's mental health.

5. As soon as the psychiatrist decides that an incompetent defendant is not dangerous, he should so inform the judge and attorneys. He should, if indicated, recommend outpatient treatment, placing the burden of opposing such medically appropriate treatment on the legal system.

By such legally responsible procedures psychiatrists can and should refuse to participate in practices which are detrimental to patients under their care. In the opinion of this committee, passive collaboration in legally ambiguous but abusive practices has been perhaps the most common failing of twentieth century psychiatry. To the extent that such passive collaboration is based on ignorance, it is our hope that this report will be helpful. We are convinced, however, that progressive reform requires more than information—it requires the willingness, the courage, and the activism of individual psychiatrists, supported by their profession, to challenge established practices whenever they are detrimental to patients entrusted to their care.

APPENDIXES

APPENDIX A:

COMPETENCY IN ENGLISH LAW: A BRIEF HISTORY

The question of competency to stand trial arose very early in the history of English law because the trial ritual required that the defendant enter some plea in his defense. The majority of individuals not pleading did so to resist death or forfeiture of property. They were not those who were deaf or psychotic, but undoubtedly those indicted for major felonies such as treason or homicide. If no plea was entered, the trial bogged down and perhaps conviction and execution were postponed or avoided.

After the *peine forte et dure* procedure described in Section 4, it was an enlightened advance when evidence that a defendant had been deaf and dumb from birth was recognized by the assumption that if speech were possible, the defendant would plead not guilty. Relatives of the defendant would then do their best to convey the necessary information to him by sign language, which apparently sufficed as an adequate degree of cooperation with counsel for the trial to proceed. Lord Hale's Pleas of the Crown [54] supports this position, which reflected the approach of the 17th century. Emphasis was on the "use of understanding," and if understanding could be conveyed by sign language, judgment and execution were carried out, although caution was urged.

From the similarity often observed between the "dumbness" of deaf mutes and that of the intellectually retarded, the analogy

[54] Matthew Hale, HISTORIA PLACITORUM CORONAE, 1736, Vol. 1, Chapter 4 cited in Walker, *op. cit.*, at note 23.

was extended in terms of the similarity of these two groups to certain "lunatics." A device of special inquest to determine whether lunacy was real or feigned was then introduced. A procedure from the civil law was borrowed in which the Chancellor issued a writ of "de lunatico inquirendo" for a jury of 12 men to decide whether a person was mentally competent to manage his own affairs.

In practice, the jury which was being empaneled to try the guilt of the accused would first decide whether the man was fit to be tried when the criminal issue was raised. The result was that a man indicted for a capital offense was remitted to prison until he could "advisedly" plea to the charge. In Hale's time (the seventeenth century), incompetency was subject to the following restrictions: (1) It was expressly limited to capital cases, (2) the accused must seem "absolutely mad," and (3) empaneling a jury for an inquest into competency was not obligatory but proceeded at the discretion of the judge.[55]

In practice, very few individuals were ever declared unfit to stand trial in England until the middle of the eighteenth century. At that time the incidence of those raising the defense of insanity in general increased, accompanied also by an increase in the number of pleas of unfitness to stand trial.[56] Presumably up to that time the issue was raised so sporadically that it was a rare event. What emerged as a result of the increased incidence of these cases anticipated subsequent developments as the legal standard in the 19th century. Attorneys began to raise the issue that their clients appeared to be incapable of attending to the evidence, or of subsequently remembering parts of it, which counsel felt to be essential to a fair trial.

Various standards relating to this lack of comprehension and memory began to emerge in different publicized trials. One of the most liberal standards was applied in the case of a flamboyant individual who, by description, appears to

[55] *Ibid.*
[56] Walker, *op. cit.*, at note 23.

have been a paranoid schizophrenic.[57] In 1790 this man threw a stone at the coach of George III as it was passing him in the street. This was a capital offense. The standard employed at the time of his trial was that no man should have his guilt determined until "by collecting together his intellects, and having them entire, he shall be able so to model his defense as to ward off the punishment of the law." [58] This text—stipulating the defendant's having all his wits together—would be more liberal in effect than that employed in most Anglo-American jurisdictions at the present time.

Out of these various trials what emerged was largely the use of commonly accepted phraseology pertaining to mental states or conditions in which there was questionable cognitive performance. However, no criteria were provided to determine what degree of mental state would indicate incompetency. Attempts were made, case by case, to make more precise the degree of insanity someone must manifest to be adjudged incompetent. As with rules for criminal responsibility, a heavy emphasis upon the cognitive prevailed. Did a defendant possess sufficient reason to understand the nature of the proceedings and conduct a defense with discretion? This emerged as a criterion in the case of a deaf mute, Esther Dyson, arraigned in 1831 for beheading her bastard child.[59] Five years later further detail was given in the case of Pritchard, indicted for bestiality.[60] The jury was to consider not only whether the defendant was of sufficient intellect to comprehend the course of the proceedings of the trial, but whether he was capable of challenging any of the jurors to whom he might object, and of comprehending the details of the evidence.

During the latter half of the 19th century there was an upsurge in the number of incompetency findings; the main causative factor appears to be connected with the nationaliza-

[57] Howell, *op. cit.* at note 24.
[58] *Ibid.*
[59] *Regina v. Dyson, op. cit.,* at note 25.
[60] Walker, *op. cit.,* at note 23.

tion of the prison system. One of the requirements of nationalization was standardization of the various local jails with regard to a prison medical officer, the gaol surgeon, who was required to see each prisoner once a week. Thus, prisoners awaiting trial were more often seen by some type of medical personnel than formerly, hence the probability of their being viewed as unfit was increased.

The prison surgeon had few or no standards to go by, and most likely was unaware of the legal reasoning employed by certain judges in reaching their opinions. The medical officers in jails adopted a standard from another context with which they were more familiar. This was the standard for civil commitment, so that, knowingly or unknowingly, the prison physicians began to equate unfitness to plead with certifiability as mentally ill. However, the criteria for certifiability had themselves never been clear beyond some reference to the patient as a danger to himself or others, or in such broad terms as someone who is insane or in need of mental treatment. In practice, therefore, the physician often fell back upon whatever opinion he had when a given individual appeared to him to be certifiable.

These vague standards of competency, so ambiguously applied, were brought to the United States, where in our legal system their application continued to generate the same degree of confusion accompanying their use in English law. Nevertheless, as one reflects on their historical evolution, two functions stand out: (1) Competency to participate in a trial was first deemed necessary so that the procedure of the trial would seem meaningful—this might be described as the ritual function; (2) competency came also to express an overriding concern that the defendant be able to protect himself in the context of the Anglo-American trial system in which he and his lawyer are seen as taking on the prosecution in an adversary struggle—this might be described as a protective or fairness function.

APPENDIX B:

CRITERIA OF COMPETENCY TO STAND TRIAL

The following checklists are intended for use by psychiatrists in providing a brief, convenient review of areas for investigation in evaluating whether a patient can be considered competent to stand trial or must be considered incompetent by reason of intellectual or mental defect.

General rule.—To be considered competent to stand trial, an individual must possess sufficient capacity to comprehend the nature and object of the proceedings and his own position in relation to those proceedings; and to be able to advise counsel rationally in the preparation and implementation of his own defense.

TABLE 1

Legal Criteria of Competency to Stand Trial *

Factual Criteria	*Inferential Criteria*
Defendant's ability to	Defendant's ability to communicate with counsel and to
1—Understand his current legal situation	7—Comprehend instructions and advice
2—Understand the charges made against him	8—Make decisions after advice
3—Understand the legal issues and procedures in his case	9—Follow testimony for contradictions or errors
4—Understand the possible dispositions, pleas, and penalties	10—Maintain a collaborative relationship with his attorney
5—Understand the facts relevant to his case	11—Testify if necessary and be cross-examined
6—Identify and locate witnesses	12—Tolerate stress at the trial or while awaiting trial
	13—Refrain from irrational behavior during the trial

* Barry A. Bukatman, J. L. Foy & Edward Degrazia, What is competency to stand trial? *American Journal of Psychiatry* 127, 9 (Mar. 1971): 1225-1229. Reproduced by permission of the authors.

TABLE 2

A Checklist of Criteria for Competency to Stand Trial [1]

Defendant's	*O.K.*	*Mental Illness* [2, 3]	*Intellectual Deficiency* [4, 5]
1. Comprehension of court proceedings [6]			
Surroundings	—	—	—
Procedure	—	—	—
Principals	—	—	—
Charges	—	—	—
Verdicts	—	—	—
Penalties	—	—	—
Legal rights	—	—	—
2. Ability to advise counsel			
Facts	—	—	—
Plea	—	—	—
Legal strategy	—	—	—
Maintaining relationship with lawyer	—	—	—
Maintaining consistency of defense			
Waiving rights	—	—	—
Interpreting witnesses' testimony	—	—	—
Testifying (if necessary)	—	—	—
3. Susceptibility to decompensation while awaiting or standing trial			
Violence	—	—	—
Acute psychosis	—	—	—
Suicidal depression	—	—	—
Agressive withdrawal	—	—	—
Organic deterioration	—	—	—

1 SOURCE: Ames Robey, M.D., Medical Director, Massachusetts Correctional Institution, Bridgewater, Massachusetts 02324, as presented at the 121st Annual Meeting of the American Psychiatric Association, 1965. Reproduced by permission of the author.

2 Includes evaluation of cognition, orientation, apperception and judgment.

3 Generally excludes character disorders.

4 Generally competent when I.Q. registers above 60 (W.A.I.S.).

5 Includes psychiatric evaluation of the nature of the charges and the complexity of the case.

6 Includes psychiatric evaluation of the court's expectations, if possible.

TABLE 3

Competency Assessment Instrument *

	Degree of Incapacity					
Capacity	*Total* (1)	*Severe* (2)	*Moderate* (3)	*Mild* (4)	*None* (5)	*Unratable* (6)
1. Appraisal of legal defenses available	—	—	—	—	—	—
2. Unmanageable behavior	—	—	—	—	—	—
3. Quality of relating to attorney	—	—	—	—	—	—
4. Planning of legal strategy, including guilty pleas to lesser charges, where pertinent	—	—	—	—	—	—
5. Appraisal of role of:						
a) Defense counsel	—	—	—	—	—	—
b) Prosecuting attorney	—	—	—	—	—	—
c) Judge	—	—	—	—	—	—
d) Jury	—	—	—	—	—	—
e) Defendant	—	—	—	—	—	—
f) Witnesses	—	—	—	—	—	—
6. Understanding of court procedure	—	—	—	—	—	—
7. Appreciation of charges	—	—	—	—	—	—
8. Appreciation of range and nature of possible penalties	—	—	—	—	—	—
9. Appraisal of likely outcomes	—	—	—	—	—	—

* A. Louis McGarry. "Competency to Stand Trial and Mental Illness," in CRIME AND DELINQUENCY ISSUES, an NIMH Monograph Series, DHEW Publication #(HSM) 73-9105 (Rockville, Md.: DHEW).

TABLE 3—Continued

Competency Assessment Instrument *

	Degree of Incapacity					
Capacity	*Total* (1)	*Severe* (2)	*Moderate* (3)	*Mild* (4)	*None* (5)	*Unratable* (6)
10. Capacity to disclose to attorney available pertinent facts surrounding the offense, including defendant's movements, timing, mental state, actions at time of offense	—	—	—	—	—	—
11. Capacity to challenge prosecution witnesses realistically	—	—	—	—	—	—
12. Capacity to testify relevantly	—	—	—	—	—	—
13. Self-defeating vs self-serving motivation (to protect himself and utilize available legal safeguards)	—	—	—	—	—	—

(Signature of Examiner)

ACKNOWLEDGMENTS TO CONTRIBUTORS

The program of the Group for the Advancement of Psychiatry, a nonprofit, tax-exempt organization, is made possible largely through the voluntary contributions and efforts of its members. For their financial assistance during the past fiscal year in helping it to fulfill its aims, GAP is grateful to the following:

Sponsors

J. Aron Charitable Foundation
Ciba-Geigy Corporation
The Division Fund
Maurice Falk Medical Fund
The Grove Foundation
The Holzheimer Fund
Ittleson Family Foundation
Merck, Sharp & Dohme
The Olin Foundation
Pfizer Laboratories
The Phillips Foundation
Roche Laboratories
Rockefeller Brothers Fund
Sandoz Pharmaceuticals
Schering Corporation
The Murray L. Silberstein Fund
The Lucille Ellis Simon Foundation
The Norton Simon Foundation
The Smart Family Foundation
Smith, Kline & French Laboratories
van Ameringen Foundation, Inc.
Leo S. Weil Foundation
Lawrence Weinberg
Weyerhaeuser Foundation, Inc.
Wyeth Laboratories

Donors

Fannie & Arnold Askin Foundation
Orrin Stine
The Stone Foundation, Inc.

OTHER PUBLICATIONS OF INTEREST
GROUP FOR THE ADVANCEMENT OF PSYCHIATRY

No.	Title	Price
87	FROM DIAGNOSIS TO TREATMENT: AN APPROACH TO TREATMENT PLANNING FOR THE EMOTIONALLY DISTURBED CHILD	$4.00
86	HUMANE REPRODUCTION	4.00
85	THE WELFARE SYSTEM AND MENTAL HEALTH	1.50
84	THE JOYS AND SORROWS OF PARENTHOOD	4.00
83	THE VIP WITH PSYCHIATRIC IMPAIRMENT	2.00
79	TOWARD A PUBLIC POLICY ON MENTAL HEALTH CARE OF THE ELDERLY	1.00
75	THE RIGHT TO ABORTION: A PSYCHIATRIC VIEW	1.00
61	LAWS GOVERNING HOSPITALIZATION OF THE MENTALLY ILL	.50
45	CONFIDENTIALITY AND PRIVILEGED COMMUNICATION IN THE PRACTICE OF PSYCHIATRY	.75

Orders amounting to less than $5.00 must be accompanied by remittance. All prices are subject to change without notice.

GAP publications may be ordered on a subscription basis. The current subscription cycle comprising the Volume VIII Series covers the period from July 1, 1971 to June 30, 1974. For further information, write the Publications Office (see below).

Bound volumes of GAP publications issued since 1947 are also available which include GAP titles no longer in print and no longer available in any other form. A bound index to these volumes (I through VII) has been published separately.

Please send your order and remittance to: Publications Office, Group for the Advancement of Psychiatry, 419 Park Avenue South, New York, New York 10016.

This publication was produced for the Group for the Advancement of Psychiatry by the Mental Health Materials Center, Inc., New York.